MW00613391

SAVE A LIFE
WHEN SECONDS COUNT

A guidebook to handle
life-threatening situations!

John Buell

"To my beautiful wife Terri.
My best friend, my inspiration and
the love of my life!"

Save A Life When Seconds Count!
© 2019 John Buell

All rights reserved. No portion of this publication may be reproduced, stored, and/or copied electronically (except for academic use as a source), nor transmitted in any form or by any means without the prior written permission of the publisher and/or author. Published in the United States of America by:

Printed in the United States.

Covers and logo design by Jack Potter of Potter Marketing & Branding

Interior layout by Darlene Swanson • van-garde.com

ISBN: 978-0-578-60239-4 (paperback)

Disclaimer:

All the information in this book is published in good faith and for general information purposes only. The book (*Save A Life When Seconds Count*) and Author (John Buell) do not make any warranties about the completeness, reliability or accuracy of this information. Any action you take upon the information you find in this book is strictly at your own risk. *Save A Life When Seconds Count* or John Buell will not be liable for any losses and/or damages in connection with the use of this book.

Contents

"What Do You Do?" Drills

Introduction

This small airplane crashed into my neighborhood and I saw the flaming black mushroom cloud rise up into the sky.

I got to the scene in less than a minute and already some teenagers were using gardens hoses to battle the fire in the backyard of the house.

The plane slammed into the roof of the house with enough force to disengage the propellor and the engine. I will never forget walking just inches from that sizzling, popping wreckage!

The impact of the crash shattered all the windows and smoke was billowing from the house. There was glass everywhere!

Expecting to see carnage in the back yard, I was shocked to see a calm scene with the pilot and co-pilot gathering their belongings and another person lying down with minor injuries.

Clearwater Fire & Rescue arrived with loud sirens so I left the scene.

I felt good for doing something "courageous" but I did nothing effective because honestly I didn't know what to do.

Factually, I put myself at risk BIG TIME! I was wearing flip-flops and shorts with no protection at all. So many hazards! Live power lines were on the ground, airplane fuel, fire, broken glass and torn metal!

It was lucky for me that I didn't get seriously injured or killed.

Later that evening I watched the news story and discovered there was another passenger in the plane! She was friend of mine from school. I never saw her at the scene of the crash. Miraculously, like the other passengers, she survived with minor injuries.

I really felt bad that I didn't do anything effective! It was a major "Wake up Call"

Wake-up Call

This incident shaped my destiny!

I decided to get trained for any emergency so I would always be ready and able to safely respond to any urgent or life-threatening situation.

Now, years after that fateful airplane crash, I have instructed hundreds of citizens on how to safely respond during an emergency to save the lives of children, adults, family and friends!

My purpose is to empower people to effectively save lives! I train SUPERHEROES!

I wrote this book because only a small percentage of the US population really know how to handle life-threatening emergency situations!

Why?

Because "American Citizens" have the idea that emergency training is the responsibility of government agencies and unfortunately government training is sometimes very poor!

It's a sober fact that our nation does not know what to do in emergency situations! The training of civilians is a missing part of Emergency Management in America and I hope to revolutionize this sector of society.

Emergency Medical Services are the heroes in our communities!

They are life-saving, highly trained and efficient!

When that call comes in: "911, What Is Your Emergency?" They go into action and save lives!

According to the Medical News Bulletin in 2017 the average response time from the 911 call until the ambulance arrives is SEVEN MINUTES!

That is the most critical time for action! This is when heroes are made! And knowing what to do instantly during a life-threatening situation is an extremely valuable skill!

I have written this book in simple terms so it can be easily understood.

My purpose is to educate thousands of people on these simple life-saving skills resulting in millions of lives saved!

I want to create prepared and resilient communities in our great nation!

If my actions can save even one single person then all my work will be worthwhile!

-John Buell
(Educator and Humanitarian)

Emergency Training and Education

I learned how to be prepared when I was a Boy Scout. The Scout motto is "Be Prepared" and my Scout Master took the time to ensure I had everything needed to be able to camp out in the wilderness. This translated into being ready for almost anything that might happen.

As an adult, I became interested in emergency response training through the Federal Emergency Management Agency (FEMA).

I did the basic training course called "CERT" the Community Emergency Response Teams. This was training to learn how to safely respond to any type of emergency or disaster. I loved it!

I attended a national training and got certified to deliver the CERT program and since then I have trained more than 250 people on this awesome program. I have also attended many trainings and CERT conventions and I have a sponsorship with a local fire station and the County Emergency Management Agency.

I recommend this program to any person interested in learning emergency and life saving skills.

The training covers preparedness, fire safety and suppression, light search and rescue, triage, medical first aid, and coordinating with government agencies.

Do You Really Know What to Do During an Emergency?

It's not something you think about unless you're a firefighter or medical responder.

The majority of citizens will do nothing more than call 911 to help their fellow man during a life-threatening emergency situation.

Most people are just spectators during these events. They don't know what to do other than call 911 or take a selfie video. And when people do attempt to rescue a victim they are likely to become victims themselves.

On the other end of the spectrum, courageous people, without hesitation, will immediately take action to help another person during an emergency. I have the greatest admiration for those who jump into action to save the life of a person they don't even know.

But unfortunately, many of these heroes are injured and sometimes they pay the ultimate price.

In this educational book I hope to bring up your awareness and ability to safely survive any type of emergency or disaster situation.

Now before we dive into all the preparedness, rescue actions and life-saving abilities, we must understand:

The Most Important Skill and Ability to Survive
Any Emergency or Disaster Situation Is:
"SITUATIONAL AWARENESS!"

Now what does that mean exactly?

It is paying attention to what is going on around you. It is the ability to calmly scan the area and see what is happening.

It means you need to look and perceive what's happening in your environment.

What is that suspicious person doing in the parking lot?

Is your home safe or is the TV about to fall over on the baby?

It is a very intelligent person that recognizes a potential emergency and safely handles the hazardous situation.

Emergency responders don't just rush in to the rescue. They make an assessment of the situation by finding out what is going on.

Is the scene safe? What happened? How many people are injured? What is the most likely outcome? Any other possible hazards like gasoline, electricity, natural gas, broken glass, propane tanks, flammable liquids or gun ammunition.

Fire fighters ALWAYS size up the scene before engaging the flames!

Have you ever heard the phrase "Know Before You Go?"

That phrase definitely applies to emergency response!

OK, now you have situational awareness of the scene so what next?

Make a plan! Then get into action and follow your plan.

Here is the sequence:

1. Situational awareness

2. Make a plan

3. Follow the plan

4. Start again with situational awareness

This is a continual process that repeats until the dangerous event is totally handled!

Has the emergency gotten better now? Are things under control?

Or is the situation getting worse?

That is the the cycle of emergency response and it applies to any emergency or disaster.

Your own awareness and the skills you will learn in this book will prepare you for any type of life-threatening emergency situation.

Seven Minutes!

About 240 million Americans dial 911 each year according to (NENA) "The National Emergency Number Association."

Researchers at the "Medical News Bulletin" found that the average time for first responders to arrive on the scene is seven minutes.

During an automobile accident or an active shooter event, that seven minutes could make the difference of life or death. Being aware of the situation and knowing what to do is a very valuable!

In this new world of mobile devices, people have their attention within a very small space. They are mostly oblivious of their surroundings!

Many people are detached from the reality and awareness of what is really going on. Instead of looking at the environment they snap a picture or make a selfie video and post it on Facebook!

A person that is trained to handle an emergency situation has a definite survival advantage. If you know the technology and procedures of emergencies then you, yourself are not likely to become the victim of an emergency.

Can you see the personal value of emergency training?

Let's take a look at the different types of life-threatening emergencies and disasters.

Natural Emergencies

Natural emergencies can happen at any time so it is best to be prepared for anything. Some natural emergencies like hurricanes and blizzards are pretty well predicted by meteorologists and the news channels.

But others like an earthquake or sinkhole can happen very quickly with devastating results.

With the recent hurricanes in Florida and Puerto Rico and the wildfires in California, we have learned to pay attention to the forecasts and take action to get to out of harms way. It's best to decide on a course of action early instead of waiting until the last minute.

Man Made Emergencies

Manmade emergencies like oil spills, the internet crashing, cyber attacks, active shooter events or nuclear threats can be hard to confront but your best prevention is to be prepared for anything!

Start stockpiling supplies of food, water and survival gear. Take some advice from a Boy Scout and remember the scout motto: Be Prepared!

Emergencies in the Home or at Work

The majority of people spend most of their time at home or at work. So let's take a look at what we can do to respond to emergency situations in the home or at the workplace.

Here's some emergencies that could occur at work or at home:

Heart Attack, Stroke, Drowning, Burns, Smoke, Poison, Drug Overdose, Dizziness, Choking, Trauma, Fainting.

So, what do you do? The answer is always the same!

1. Stay calm!

2. Call 911

3. Follow the instructions of the 911 Operator.

Poison Emergencies

Prevention is the most important consideration in the handling of poison emergencies. Obviously you keep poisonous substances and medications locked in a secure cabinet. Ensure all medicines have correct labels and child-resistant packages.

Household cleaners should also be stored in locked cabinets and out of the reach of children and pets.

Usually a poison emergency is the result of an accident but unfortunately many times poison emergencies occur as an attempt to commit suicide.

Poison emergencies definitely include drug overdose and excess alcohol or toxic situations.

Here's the handling for a poison emergency:

- If the person is unconscious, having convulsions or any difficulty breathing, call 911.
- Otherwise call the Poison Control Center at 1-800-222-1222.
- Be ready to answer questions:
- Age and weight of the person?
- What was swallowed or inhaled?
- How much was taken?
- How is the person is doing right now?
- Follow the instructions from Poison Control or the 911 Operator.

Keeping Children Safe from Emergencies

Children are at risk for injuries and emergencies because they don't have full control of their bodies. Infants are totally dependent upon Mom or Dad or another family member or caretaker. Toddlers are very curious and love to explore. So it is extremely important to make your home safe.

Do a very complete safety checklist including:

- Small toys - choking hazard
- Stoves
- Electrical outlets
- Water temperature settings
- Windows and shades
- Stairs
- Cabinets
- Cleaning supplies
- Sharp edges
- Slippery floors
- Carpets
- Furniture
- Lock drawers and doors

Obviously, the safety of your children is the top priority at home so create a safe environment and let them play and have fun.

Emergencies with the Elderly

Older adults have difficulties due to their frailty and advancing years.

If the elderly person is living alone they should always have a cell phone and a Medical Alert System. You've seen the TV commercial of the elderly lady screaming "I've fallen and I can't get up!"

These systems are life savers!

Just like with children, seniors need a safe environment with minimal hazards.

Arrange for someone to check in with the person on a regular basis.

Senior citizens should also establish a support network of family members, close friends, neighbors, caregivers and doctors.

Being prepared for any emergency is essential in the senior community. Ensure they have water and food supplies for at least 3 days and make sure they have the address to the nearest emergency shelter.

Pet Emergencies

Many people value the lives of their pets more than life itself!

Personally, I would do everything possible to rescue my dog Blackjack if he was in trouble. But I would also make sure the scene was safe before I took action.

I love animals and I always try to stop to rescue a pet or wild animal. I have successfully reunited many lost dogs and cats with their masters.

As always, you should be prepared for emergencies and that includes pets. In addition to your emergency kit for humans, put together first aid supplies and survival items for your pet including:

1. Extra water

2. Extra dog food

3. Bowl for water and food

4. Carrier for you pet

5. Leash

6. Muzzle if needed

7. Thick gloves

8. Towel or blanket

9. Your pet's favorite toy

10. First aid items for your pet (Bandages, pet prescriptions, oint-

ments and medications)

11. Also write down the address and phone number of your veterinarian clinic or animal hospital.

911 Emergency calls are only for humans so definitely have a good relationship with your vet.

Automobile Emergencies

As a driver or passenger, an automobile is actually a very dangerous place to be. The National Safety Council reports an estimated 40,000 people lost their lives in car crashes on US roads in 2017.

The most telling statistic is the skyrocketing injuries and fatalities from "distractive driving" and the use of cell phones while driving.

It is an epidemic in the US.

The statistics tell the staggering story!

- More than 90 people die in car accidents every day.
- Average number of car accidents in the U.S. every year is 6 million.
- 1 in 7 people do not wear a seatbelt while driving.
- Seatbelts reduce the risk of death by 45%.
- Seatbelts cut the risk of serious injury by 50%.
- People not wearing a seatbelt are 30 times more likely to be ejected from the vehicle during a crash.
- Crashes result in:
- 6% Fatality
- 27% Non-fatality injury
- 72% Property damage
- Typical Causes of Accidents that Result in Death:
- Alcohol 40%

- Speeding 30%

- Reckless Driving 33%

- Distracted Driving

- Each day, more than 9 people are killed due to distracted driving.

- More than 1060 people are injured in crashes that involve a distracted driver.

- And 1 out of 3 people text while driving.

- You are 23 times more likely to crash while texting while driving.

- Distraction was reported as a factor in nearly 1 in 5 crashes in which someone was injured.

- 40% of all American teens say that they have been in a car when the driver used a cell phone in a way that put people in danger.

- Driving while using a cell phone reduces the amount of brain activity associated with driving by 37%.

- Sending or receiving a text takes a driver's eyes from the road for an average of 4.6 seconds, the equivalent of driving the length of an entire football field blind.

The moral of this story is: Pay attention when you are driving and don't allow ANY type of distractions!

When Approaching an Emergency Scene On a Road or Highway

When approaching the emergency scene slow down and move over to allow emergency vehicles to get past. This is the law in all 50 states.

Stay in your vehicle and keep your seat belts on.

Be alert for any other emergency vehicles and check your rearview mirror to see what's happening behind you. Obviously, turn off the music and get off the cell phone.

Always follow the responders instructions and don't be a spectator while driving by.

The 3 Killers

There are three major categories of situations that can result in death. Airway, bleeding and shock. Paramedics and firefighters respond every day to hundreds of emergency situations. Some of them are medical related and others from injuries and physical trauma. Car crashes, job related incidents, illnesses and accidents can result in life threatening situations. Remember that the average response time from the emergency responders is seven minutes. Knowing what to do in these situations is a very valuable life-saving skill. Seven minutes might be too long! You may be the one to save the day!

Airway

If a person is unable to breathe in oxygen, they will go unconscious and eventually die.

According to the National Safety Council, thousands of people die from choking every year. About half of those victims were elderly.

Usually it happens when a person is eating.

If you see someone clutching their throat, coughing, gagging, wheezing or passed out, would you know what to do?

The "Heimlich Maneuver" has been around for years and has been the recommended technique for a choking victim.

Here is the technique:

- If a person is coughing forcefully, encourage continued coughing to clear the object.

- A person who can't cough, speak or breathe, however, needs immediate help. Ask if they are choking and let them know you will use abdominal thrusts, also known as the Heimlich maneuver, to prevent suffocation. The procedure is not recommended for children younger than 1.

- Stand behind the victim with one leg forward between the victim's legs.

- For a child, move down to their level and keep your head to one side.

- Reach around the abdomen and locate the navel.

- Place the thumb side of your fist against the abdomen just above the navel.

- Grasp your fist with your other hand and thrust inward and upward into the victim's abdomen with quick jerks.

- For a responsive pregnant victim, or any victim you cannot get your arms around or for whom abdominal thrusts are not effective, give chest thrusts from behind; avoid squeezing the ribs with your arms.

- Continue thrusts until the victim expels the object or becomes unresponsive.

- Even after choking stops, seek medical attention.

Knowing what to do when a person is choking can save the life of a friend or family member.

Bleeding

If a person is bleeding heavily and the blood isn't stopped, they will die.

Pressure combined with elevation will address most bleeding.

Step 1: Place direct pressure over the wound by putting a clean bandage over the wound and pressing firmly.

Step 2: Maintain pressure on the bandage over the wound until the bleeding stops. If necessary, put on another bandage on top of the first one and keep the pressure on.

Step 3: If possible, elevate the body part above the heart.

Shock

The most misunderstood of these three killers is "shock" so let's get this defined. It isn't that you got surprised or you put your finger in a light socket.

Shock is a life-threatening medical condition as a result of insufficient blood flow throughout the body. It is an indication that something is very wrong and requires immediate action.

If the condition of "shock" isn't handled rapidly a person can also die. The symptoms of shock are:

Rapid and shallow breathing. Cool, clammy skin, pale skin, rapid breathing, nausea or vomiting, enlarged pupils, weakness or fatigue, dizziness or fainting, or failing to follow a simple command like "Can you lift up your right hand?"

The handling for shock is:

1. Call 911 Emergency Services.
2. Lay the victim on his or her back.
3. Elevate the feet 6 to 10 inches above the level of the heart.
4. Maintain an open airway.
5. Control obvious bleeding.
6. Maintain body temperature. Cover the ground and the victim with a blanket if necessary.
7. Avoid rough and excessive handling.

Recognizing a person in shock and doing this rapid treatment can save a life. It's good to know how to handle this type of critical situation. What if it was a friend or family member?

Person Too Cold - Hypothermia

HYPO means: "Under, Down, Beneath"

THERMIA means: "Generating Heat"

Hypothermia is a medical emergency that occurs when the body is not generating enough heat. The person is too cold and this is also a life-threatening situation.

The first obvious symptom is shivering. Shivering is the body's response to warm up the body. Your body is telling you that you should get out of the cold and go inside to get warm.

The treatment for hypothermia:

- Be gentle with the person.
- Get them into a warm place.
- Remove any wet clothing.
- Cover the person with blankets.
- Give them some warm beverages.

Person Too Hot - Hyperthermia

HYPER means: "Too Much"

THERMIA means: "Generating Heat"

Hyperthermia means the person is dangerously too hot.

It is a medical emergency condition that occurs when the body is too hot and this is a life-threatening situation.

Simply put, if a person is too hot they could die.

The human body has a pretty small range of tolerable temperatures.

The normal human body temperature is about 98 degrees Fahrenheit. (37 Celsius)

Heat emergency situations have three stages: Heat cramps, heat exhaustion, and heatstroke. All three stages of heat emergency are serious.

Symptoms of Hyperthermia:

- Throbbing headache.

- Dizziness and light-headedness.

- Lack of sweating despite the heat.

- Red, hot, and dry skin.

- Muscle weakness or cramps.

- Nausea and vomiting.

- Rapid heartbeat, which may be either strong or weak.

- Rapid, shallow breathing.

Treatment for Hyperthermia:

- Cool the person as fast as you can!

- Get the person into a cool place.

- Remove clothes.

- Immerse the person in cold water.

- Drink fluids like water or sports drinks.

- Cool the person as fast as you can!

- Get the person into a cool place.

- Remove clothes.

- Immerse the person in cold water.

- Drink fluids like water or sports drinks.

Heart Attack

Heart disease and heart attacks are the most major cause of death in the United States! According to the American Heart Association in 2017, approximately 800,000 deaths occurred in the United States from heart related problems.

70% of heart attacks occur in the home.

The most common symptom of a heart attack is chest pain.

Other symptoms include: pressure in the chest, shortness of breath, dizziness, cold sweat, fatigue.

A heart attack is the result of a clogged artery. The heart becomes damaged without the blood flow to the heart. At that point the heart muscle begins to die.

It is CRITICAL to handle this situation as fast as possible!

If you suspect the person is having a heart attack, call 911 and immediately alert Emergency Medical Services.

Keep the person comfortable until emergency medical services arrive.

Many people survive heart attacks with fast response and medical treatment.

Note: You don't do CPR on a heart attack victim because the heart is still pumping. The problem is the flow of blood is BLOCKED.

Sudden Cardiac Arrest

Let's define these terms because this emergency is a major killer!

It is different from a heart attack.

Sudden = Occurring quickly and unexpectedly or without warning

Cardiac = Relating to the heart

Arrest = To stop

Cardiac arrest means literally that the heart has suddenly stopped! The person is dead.

Sudden Cardiac Arrest is the leading cause of death in America with 325,000 per year according to the Sudden Cardiac Arrest Foundation. That's about 1000 people every day!

The person in cardiac arrest is technically dead but the good news is that sometimes the person can be brought back to life!

I'm sure you have heard about CPR.

Let's define these words:

CPR = Cardio Pulmonary Resuscitation

Cardio means: "relating to the heart"

Pulmonary means: "relating to the lungs"

Resuscitation means: "to bring something back to life"

CPR is a life-saving technique to bring a person back from the dead.

If a person's heart is not pumping blood and they are not breathing then they are technically dead.

CPR can possibly save the life of someone you love.

How valuable is that?

In recent years, emergency responders and medical experts have discovered that many more lives can be saved with fast action and just doing chest compressions without "Mouth to Mouth" rescue breathing.

If a person suddenly falls down with Cardiac Arrest then it's best to keep the blood moving through the body. The idea is that the victim has some oxygen already inside his body and that oxygen is moving to the brain and keeping the victim alive.

Hands-Only CPR is now standard technique for sudden cardiac arrest and it doesn't require "Mouth-To-Mouth" rescue breathing.

The technique is very simple:

- Check to see if the victim is responsive. Tap the shoulder and ask "Are you OK?"

- If the person is not responding and shows no signs of life - Call 911 or get another person to call 911.

- Get the victim flat on the back.

- Start Hands-Only CPR

- Position yourself over the victim.

- Lock your arms straight.

- Push hard and fast! 2 inches deep in the middle of the chest about 100 beats per minute.

- 100 beats per minute is the tempo of the Bee-Gees song "Stayin' Alive."

There is also an electronic device that has saved millions of people!

They use very big words to describe this but I'll do my best to explain.

The heart beats in a rhythm by a steady electrical process that keeps the heart pumping regularly.

During Sudden Cardiac Arrest the electrical system in the heart freaks out and starts jiggling like a bowl of quivering jelly.

The heart stops pumping and just quivers. The technical word to describe this heart condition is: Fibrillation. At that point the heart is not pumping. The person is dead.

Defibrillation is the action of resetting the heart's electrical system similar to using a "Jump Start" when your car has a dead battery.

An AED machine (Automated External Defibrillator) delivers an electrical shock that can bring the person back to life and reset the regular beat of the heart.

AED machines are automated. That means that the machine is running the show although a rescuer needs to open it up and turn it on. The AED has a speaker and it tells you EXACTLY what to do! Follow the directions and hopefully you will safe a life!

Millions of people have been saved with CPR, AED and the heroes that took action to save another's life!

Emergency Preparedness

At the very least, the Department of Homeland Security recommends you have a basic emergency supply kit that includes enough food and water for each of your family members for 72 hours. That's 1 gallon of water per day per person and canned or otherwise nonperishable food for three days.

However, it's a good idea to stockpile some beans and rice. And get a good water filter to ensure you can have drinkable water. Camping and fishing gear is also a great thing to have at home just in case you need to cook some food and stay warm.

I keep a backpack in the trunk of my car packed with emergency supplies, tools, rope, fishing gear and survival food.

Emergency Drilling

Get the family together have some fun drilling safely getting out of the home. Decide where you will meet outside if there is an actual fire. Then go to the bedrooms of the house and act like you're sleeping. Then Mom or Dad will test the smoke alarm and everybody quickly and safely get out of the house. Then join up at your designated place. Do this drill each month and remember also to regularly change the batteries in the smoke alarms. Schools routinely run fire drills and smart businesses have an emergency plan that includes periodic fire drills.

Emergency Planning

Make copies of your valuable documents: drivers licenses, passports, birth certificates, and other valuable documents like Insurance policies, automobile titles, stocks and bonds, medical records. Etc. Also, make a printout of all of your phone contacts.

Emergency Shelter Locations

Decide early if you are going to evacuate or shelter in place.

Follow the warnings and instructions from government officials.

If you are going to stay, then secure doors and windows.

Acquire sand bags if necessary.

Find out the shelter locations in your area and be ready to get to a safe shelter location.

Make arrangements for your pets.

Escaping a Fire

Every year thousands of people are killed in home fires. It's a very real problem! That's why you must know how to get out of the burning building quickly. Here are some important tips:

Smoke detectors saves lives!

You won't escape if you don't have adequate warning! So the first rule is to install smoke detectors outside every sleeping area and on each floor. Remember to check the batteries often. The best way is to make a room by room layout of your home with all emergency exits clearly shown. Make sure all members of the family know and understand exactly what to do and where to go in an emergency.

Make sure there is more than one exit from every room.

Practice getting out of the house fast and getting to the meeting place.

Smoke is usually poisonous and hot! Crawl low under the smoke!

Never use an elevator during a fire escape.

Get out as quickly as you can and don't stop for pets or possessions.

And never go back inside! Once you are safely out, stay out!

Using a Fire Extinguisher

Here are the steps to put out a small fire with the fire extinguisher.

Using your skill of situational awareness, observe the scene and determine if it is safe to put out the fire using a fire extinguisher.

Ensure you have more than 2 ways to exit the scene.

Approach the fire from upwind to avoid the smoke and heat.

Ensure that you have the correct fire extinguisher for that type of fire. Put out a fire using the P.A.S.S. method.

- **PULL** (You pull out the pin).
- **AIM** (You aim the fire extinguisher nozzle at the base of the fire).
- **SQUEEZE** (You squeeze the fire extinguisher trigger).
- **SWEEP** (You sweep from side to side at the base of the fire).

Most fire extinguishers in the home are ABC -Type.

Type A fires are ordinary things that burn like paper or wood.

Type B fires are flammable liquids like gasoline.

Type C fires are energized equipment like a toaster.

ABC fire extinguishers are designed to handle A, B and C Fires.

Here are the steps to put out a small fire with the fire extinguisher. Using your skill of situational awareness, observe the scene and determine if it is safe to put out the fire using a small fire extinguisher.

Ensure you have more than 2 ways exit the scene.

Approach the fire from upwind to avoid the smoke and heat.

Ensure that you have the correct fire extinguisher for that type of fire.

1. Pull the pin.
2. Aim the nozzle.
3. Squeeze the trigger.
4. Sweep at the base of the fire and put out the fire completely.

The Good Samaritan Law

A Good Samaritan is a kindly person who helps another in difficulty or distress.

Good Samaritan Laws protect people who selflessly jump in to help without the expectation of a reward.

But in our litigation-happy society you can be sued for anything!

You, as a rescuer, should always ask permission before assisting a victim.

Simply asking: "I'm trained on first aid. Is it OK for me to help you?"

If the person says: "yes" then help them as best you can until emergency responders arrive.

If the person says no, then don't attempt to help them.

If a victim is unconscious or unresponsive then it is assumed the person agrees to be helped.

This is the "reasonable man" standard.

The law assumes that a reasonable person would want medical care in an emergency.

All 50 states have some type of Good Samaritan Laws so go ahead and do your best to save a life!

A Choking Person

According to "Injury Facts" in 2017, choking is the fourth leading cause of unintentional injury death.

If you see someone clutching their throat, coughing, gagging, wheezing or passed out, would you know what to do?

The traditional rescue for a choking victim is the "Heimlich Maneuver" because Mr. Heimlich invented the procedure.

Now it is called: "Abdominal Thrusts" because you thrust (push hard) in the area of the abdomen (stomach area).

Here's what you do:

- If the person is coughing, he's getting air so encourage him to keep coughing.
- If the person cannot talk, cough or breathe then ask the person if they are actually choking. If so, call 911 and get permission to help them and start with back blows and abdominal thrusts.
- Stand behind the person. Place one foot slightly in front of the other for balance. Wrap your arms around the waist. Tip forward slightly.
- Using the heel of your other hand deliver five back blows between the shoulder blades.
- If that doesn't clear the airway then give 5 abdominal thrusts by positioning your fist slightly above the person's navel. You can ask them to point to the naval.

- Grasp the fist with the other hand. Press hard into the abdomen with a quick, upward thrust — as if trying to lift the person up.

- Perform 5 quick abdominal thrusts.

- Repeat the back blows and abdominal thrusts until the airway is clear or the person becomes unconscious.

- Help the person to the ground if the person becomes unconscious.

- You may need to kneel down for a child that is choking and don't do very heavy back blows.

Burns

Burns really hurt! Even the small burns are very painful!

Listen to your Mom and "Don't Play With Fire!"

Pay attention with children in the kitchen and educate your little kids about the hot water in the bathtub or shower.

Here's how to treat most minor burns:

- Stop the burning! Put out the flames or remove the person from the source of the burn.

- Cool the burn using large amounts of cool water until the pain eases.

- Don't use ice.

- Cover the burn then use a dry, sterile bandage or a clean cloth to cover a burn.

- If it is a major burn then call 911.

Amputation

Even the thought of an Amputation is gruesome!

For the victim it can be terrorizing but you may be saving the life of a friend or family member.

The good news is that, with modern surgical procedures, many body parts can be successfully reattached.

Car accidents are the leading cause of amputations.

In this type of situation you need to treat the victim and also the severed body part. Obviously it is most important to save the person's life as a first action then take steps to care for the amputated body part.

Here's what to do:
- Ensure the scene is safe.
- Call 911.
- Stop the bleeding using direct pressure with bandages.
- Treat the victim for shock.
- Calm the person as much as possible until medical help arrives.

Here's what to do with amputated body part:
- Rinse with clean water.
- Don't use soap or scrub.

- Place in a clean plastic bag.

- Pack the bag in ice.

- Take it with you to the hospital or give it to emergency responders when they arrive.

Active Shooter Event

Recently, the active shooter event has been a very hot topic in Emergency Management communities. These events are tragic and involve the entire community.

The basic actions to take during an active shooter event:

1. Run! - Run away from the area and get to a safe place.

2. Hide! - If you can't run away then hide. Lock doors, be quiet, silence mobile devices, barricade yourself in with walls and furniture.

3. Fight! - As a last resort: Kick, scratch, poke his eyes out, take him down permanently! Use anything you can as a weapon: A fire extinguisher, paperweight, hot coffee, baseball bat or pepper spray. Your best way to prepare for an active shooter event is to drill it!

How To Escape a Sinking Car

If you end up in a car that is sinking in deep water, there is a specific procedure to survive the situation.

Just considering the event is terrifying! But let's take a look at the standard procedure to save lives.

What do you do?

Try to remain calm.

Think only about quickly getting out of the car.

Don't try to call 911! Just get out!

You have about 1 minute to get everyone out of the vehicle!

Unbuckle your seatbelt, roll down the windows then get out!

Don't try to open the doors. They will not open because of the water pressure.

You will need to get out through the windows. The power windows should still be working. Roll them down.

If the windows don't roll down you must break them! Use anything you can to break the windows. You can buy an emergency tool to keep in your car. It's like a tiny hammer that will shatter windows.

Don't try to break the front windshield. It is super strong and it won't shatter.

If there are children in the car then get them all out of the vehicle. If possible, get older kids out first so they can help the little ones.

Remember: Seatbelts, Windows, Children, Out!

Save A Life

Emergency Training

"What Do You Do?" Drills

This book and the "Save A Life Emergency Training Drills" will revolutionize the training of citizens.

The method of study and exact drilling accomplishes CERTAINTY and instantly knowing what to do in emergency situations.

The accent is on ability with the result of total confidence.

Graduates know what to do!

They don't "remember," they just KNOW what to do.

This is something new! It is refreshing! It Works!

Three Levels Of Training

1. Read The Book.
2. Do The Sequence Drills With Another Person.
3. Attend Live Events (Hands-On Training).

Three Levels of Training

1. Read The Book.

2. Do The Sequence Drills With Another Person.

3. Attend Live Events (Hands-On Training).

Save A Life Emergency Training - Sequence Drills

Here's how the "What Do You Do" drills work:

Two people work together doing the drills.

One will be the "Student" and the other will be the "Coach."

The Coach says: "Start" and the student does the drill by saying each step in sequence. It doesn't need to be the exact wording. The student just needs to name each step in the correct sequence.

For example:

Person In Shock Drill
What Do You Do?

4. Ensure the scene is safe.

5. Call 911 or get someone else to make the call.

6. Lay the victim on his or her back.

7. Elevate the feet 6 to 10 inches above the level of the heart.

8. Maintain body temperature (Cover the ground and the victim with a blanket if possible).

If the student does the drill correctly, the coach says: PASS!

If the student does NOT do the drill correctly, the coach says: Flunk!

And the coach tells the student what he did incorrect.

Then the coach again says "Start."

They continue until the student does the drill correctly and the coach says "PASS!"

Then they do a TURNABOUT with the Coach now becoming the Student.

This method of drilling is a very effective!

1   Drill: Awareness of the emergency scene.

What Do You Do?

1. Look around and see what is happening. Don't rush in!

2. Assess the situation. Is the scene safe?

3. Make a plan to rescue the victims.

4. Follow your plan.

5. Safely rescue the victims.

2   Drill: Escape from a burning house or building.

What Do You Do?

1. Prepare for fire by ensuring smoke alarms and sprinkler systems are working properly.

2. Prepare in advance a safe place to meet outside the house or building. (The mailbox, a tree, a streetlight)

3. Quickly look around and see what is happening.

4. Quickly make a plan to get out of the building.

5. Follow your plan and get out of the burning building.

6. Go to your designated safe meeting place.

7. Call 911.

8. Don't stop to get any of your stuff.

9. Never, ever, go back into the house.

#3   Drill: Using a fire extinguisher to put out a small fire.

What Do You Do?

1. **PULL** (Pull out the extinguisher pin).

2. **AIM** (Aim the fire extinguisher nozzle at the base of the fire).

3. **SQUEEZE** (Squeeze the fire extinguisher trigger).

4. **SWEEP** (Sweep from side to side at the base of the fire).

#4 Good Samaritan Law
"Ask Permission" Drill

What do you do?
- Approach the victim.
- Ask: "Is it OK for me to help you?".
- If "yes" then treat the victim.
- If "no" then do not touch the victim.
- If the person is unconscious then consider the victim would want help and begin treatment.

#5   Choking Victim Drill

What do you do?

Rescue a choking victim using the "Act Fast Anti-Choking Trainer"

This life-saving training device was developed by Dr. Timothy Adams, MD to dislodge an object in a person's throat or airway. Training with this vest has saved thousands of lives.

1. Pull the vest on, cinch the waist belt and drop a foam plug into the 'airway'.

2. Place your hands in the correct position, between the navel and rib cage.

3. Deliver quick, upward Abdominal Thrust Maneuver (Heimlich).

4. The Act Fast Anti Choking trainer can be used standing, sitting, on the ground or even for choking self-rescue by using a counter or chair.

#6   Burn Victim Drill

What do you do?

1. Ensure the scene is safe.

2. Approach the victim.

3. Get permission to help the victim.

4. Remove the body part from the source of burning heat.

5. Using a bucket of water, cool the burn.

6. Keep cooling the burn until the victim has relief from the pain.

7. Cover the burned area with a clean cloth or sterile bandage.

#7   Bleeding Person Drill

What do you do?

1. Ensure the scene is safe.

2. Call 911 or get someone else to make the call.

3. Approach the bleeding victim and get permission to help them.

4. Put direct pressure on the wound using a bandage or clean towel.

5. Keep pressure on the body part until until you have stopped the bleeding.

6. If necessary, apply an additional bandage or towel and don't peek at the wound to see if the blood stopped.

7. Now elevate the wound above the level of the heart.

#8 Person In Shock Drill

What Do You Do?

1. Call 911 or get someone else to make the call.

2. Lay the victim on his or her back.

3. Elevate the feet 6 to 10 inches above the level of the heart.

4. Maintain body temperature (Cover the ground and the victim with a blanket if possible).

#9   Overheated Person Drill

What Do You Do?

1. Call 911 or get someone else to make the call.

2. Cool the person as fast as you can!

3. Get the person into a cool place.

4. Remove clothes.

5. Immerse the person in cold water.

6. Get the victim to drink fluids like water or sports drinks.

#10   Person Too Cold Drill

What Do You Do?

1. Call 911 or get someone else to make the call.

2. Be gentile with the person.

3. Get them into a warm place.

4. Remove any wet clothing.

5. Cover the person with blankets.

6. Give them some warm beverages.

#11 Heart Attack Drill

What Do You?

1. You observe that the person has signs of a heart attack.

2. Call 911 or get someone else to make the call.

3. Get permission to help the victim.

4. Ask the victim questions about his symptoms, any medications they are taking, and when they last ate food or water.

5. Then keep the person comfortable until the ambulance arrives.

#12   Sudden Cardiac Arrest Drill

What Do You Do?

1. Ensure the scene is safe.

2. Approach the victim, tap the shoulder and ask: "Are you OK?"

3. Recognize the victim is not responding and is not breathing.

4. Start Hands-Only CPR doing chest compressions until first responders arrive or if the victim comes back to life.

5. Get someone else to call 911.

6. Send another person to find an AED machine.

#13   Amputation Drill

What Do You Do?

1. Make sure the scene is safe.

2. Call 911 or get someone else to make the call.

3. Handle bleeding with direct pressure using bandages.

4. Treat for shock: Lift legs up above the heart and cover the person with a blanket to keep them warm.

5. Calm the person as much as possible until medical help arrives

6. Rinse the body part in water.

7. Place the body part in a clean plastic bag.

8. Pack the plastic bag in ice.

9. Give the body part to emergency responders when they arrive.

#14 Active Shooter Event Drill

What Do You Do?

The basic actions to take during an active shooter event:

1. Run! - Run away from the area and get to a safe place.

2. Hide! - If you can't run away then hide. Lock doors, be quiet, silence mobile devices, barricade yourself in with walls and furniture.

3. Fight! - As a last resort: Kick, scratch, poke his eyes out, take him down permanently! Use anything you can as a weapon: A fire extinguisher, paperweight, hot coffee, baseball bat or pepper spray.

#15   Surviving a Sinking Car Underwater Drill

What Do You Do?

If you end up in a car that is sinking in deep water, here's what to do:

1. Try to remain calm.

2. Unbuckle seatbelts.

3. Roll down the car windows - break them if they don't open.

4. Get everyone out of the car - children first.

5. Swim to safety.

Glossary of Terms

AED
An AED machine (Automated External Defibrillator) delivers an electrical shock that can bring the person back to life and reset the regular beat of the heart.

Airway:
The passageway air travels from the mouth to the lungs to allow breathing.

Alert:
To pay attention and be watchful.

Amputation
The action of cutting off a limb. (Arm, Leg, Finger or other limbs)

Ambulatory:
Able to walk around.

Assess:
To analyze and determine the significance or importance of something.

Attend:
To take charge of something and get it taken care of.

Biological:
Having to do with life or living organisms.

Blanch Test:
Blanch means to turn something white. The blanch test is done by squeezing the tip of a persons finger and looking at how long it takes for the finger to return back to the color of red or pink. You use this test during medical triage. If it takes more than 2 seconds for the finger to return to a normal red or pink color then there is a problem with circulation which indicates they may be going into shock. They would become an "Immediate" for medical treatment.

Casualty:
Someone who has been injured or killed.

CBRNE:
An acronym for weapons of mass destruction: (Chemical, Biological, Radiological, Nuclear and Explosives).

Emergency Response Kit:
The kit that has your supplies for responding to an emergency - personal protection equipment, first aid supplies, gloves, etc.

Cardiac Arrest
Also called Sudden Cardiac Arrest. Cardiac arrest means literally that the heart has suddenly stopped. It is the leading cause of death in the US.

CPR = Cardio Pulmonary Resuscitation
CPR is a life-saving technique to bring a person back from the

dead.

Cardio means: relating to the heart.

Pulmonary means relating to the lungs.

Resuscitation means to bring something back to life.

Civil Defense:
Civil means it's about people. Civil defense is simply the defense of the citizens.

Combustibles:
Something that will catch on fire and burn.

Community:
A group of people living in the same area or having similar interests.

Cribbing:
A technique for rescuing a person tapped under a heavy object by using blocks of wood to gradually lift and support the heavy object so the person can be freed.

Defibrillation
The heart beats in a rhythm by a steady electrical process that keeps the heart pumping regularly.

During Sudden Cardiac Arrest the electrical system in the heart freaks out and starts jiggling like a bowl of quivering jelly.

The heart stops pumping and just quivers. The technical word to describe this heart condition is: Fibrillation. At that point the heart is not pumping. The person is dead.

Defibrillation is the action of resetting the heart's electrical system similar to using a "Jump Start" when your car has a dead battery.

Disaster:
An event that causes great destruction, distress or misfortune.

Disaster Kit:
A kit that is prepared in advance to be used in the event of an actual disaster containing supplies that may be needed for survival. It is also called a survival kit.

Emergency:
A serious situation that develops suddenly and unexpectedly and demands immediate attention.

Endangered:
To expose to danger or harm.

Evacuate:
To purposely leave an area that might be dangerous.

Explosives:
Stuff that is used to blow up something.

Extinguisher:
To extinguish means to put out, to end or to destroy. The correct fire extinguisher should end or put out a fire.

Extrication:

To be freed from a difficult situation.

Fibrillation
During Sudden Cardiac Arrest the electrical system in the heart freaks out and starts jiggling like a bowl of quivering jelly.

The heart stops pumping and just quivers. The technical word to describe this heart condition is: Fibrillation. At that point the heart is not pumping. The person is dead.

Defibrillation is the action of resetting the heart's electrical system similar to using a "Jump Start" when your car has a dead battery.

Good Samaritan:
A compassionate person who unselfishly helps others.

Heart Attack:
A life-threatening situation as a result of a clogged artery. The heart gets damaged (attacked) because there is not enough blood flow. The problem is the flow of blood is BLOCKED.

Hazard:
A possible source of danger.

Incident Command System (ICS):
The organizational system used by all other emergency responders. The US Federal Government, State Governments, Fire Departments and Police all use the Incident Command System when responding

to an emergency. Abbreviation: ICS

Logistics:
The methods of obtaining, transporting, distributing, maintaining and replacing materials and personnel, as in a military operation or disaster response.

Mannequin:
A dummy used to display clothes in a store window.

Nuclear:
Having to do with the nucleus of an atom.

Pandemic:
An illness that spreads that expands over a large geographical area.

Perfusion:
The action of blood returning to the capillaries (smallest blood vessels). If you squeeze the end of your finger then let go, you will notice that it turns white then quickly returns to red or pink. Perfusion is a word to describe the blood returning to the area.

Psychology:
A field of study that attempts to explain mental processes and behavior. It is presented as a "Science" but is not based on factual scientific data.

Radiological:
Having to do with radiation.

Rescue:

To save from danger.

Respiration:

The act of breathing.

Response:

Taking action based on something that has happened.

Shelter:

Something that provides cover or protection.

Shock:

A very serious medical situation where the body begins to shut down and circulation of blood becomes ineffective.

Situational Awareness:

It is paying attention to what is going on around you. It is the ability to calmly scan the area and see what is happening. It means you need to look and perceive what's happening in your environment.

Size Up:

To look at something and make an estimate or judgment of a situation.

Suppression:

To put an end to something. To hold something back, push it down or restrain it.

Team:

A group of people who are working together toward a common purpose. A good team has a tendency to know what the other team members are doing and thinking and they coordinate well with each other.

Terrorism:

The use of terror, violence and intimidation to create fear.

Trauma:

A major body injury caused by sudden external violence or impact.

Triage:

The process of determining the priority of patient treatments based on how bad their injury is. It is a French word that means "To Sort". In Medical Triage you are sorting the victims based on how badly they are injured to determine how urgent they need treatment.

Made in the USA
Columbia, SC
09 November 2019

82968834R00055